Toccata and Fugue in D Minor
and the Other Bach Transcriptions
for Solo Piano

FERRUCCIO BUSONI

DOVER PUBLICATIONS, INC.
GARDEN CITY, NEW YORK

Bibliographical Note

This Dover edition, first published in 1996, is a new compilation of piano transcriptions originally published separately. *Präludium und Fuge D-dur, Orgel-Toccata d-moll, Chaconne d-moll* and *Orgel-Choralvorspiele,* Heft I/II, were originally published by Breitkopf & Härtel, Wiesbaden, n.d. Their "EB" (Edition Breitkopf) numbers are, respectively, 3355, 1372, 2334 and 2459/2460. *Toccata in C major* was originally published as Vol. 1628 of Schirmer's Library of Musical Classics by G. Schirmer, Inc., "published 1942." *Prelude and Fugue in E-flat (Praeludium und Fuge Es dur)* was originally published in an unidentified authoritative edition, n.d.

The Dover edition adds: a Publisher's Note, list of contents, glossary and English headings throughout. English translations have also been provided for footnotes on pp. 15 and 17.

International Standard Book Number

ISBN-13: 978-0-486-29050-8
ISBN-10: 0-486-29050-6

Manufactured in the United States by LSC Communications
4500050308
www.doverpublications.com

Publisher's Note

THIS EDITION contains Ferruccio Busoni's complete concert transcriptions for solo piano of compositions by Johann Sebastian Bach. Except for two works, the original compositions were written for organ—thus such alternate titles often associated with this music, even in their version for piano, as "Organ Toccata," "Organ Chorale-Prelude" and so on.

The two exceptions are the "Chaconne" from *Partita II for* [Solo] *Violin*, and the chorale-prelude "Wachet auf, ruft uns die Stimme," originally the fourth movement of the church cantata of the same name, scored for small instrumental ensemble, then later arranged for organ (not by Bach) for publication.

The term "transcription" is used in this edition to label a musical transformation, often of a virtuoso nature, for concert purposes. Busoni, however, uses that term only once, to describe his piano scores of the *Organ Chorale-Preludes*— "transcribed for the piano in chamber style." In his note to the Breitkopf edition of these works [originally in German, freely translated here], he explains:

> The style of the arrangement, which we have called "chamber style" in contrast to the "concert arrangements," only seldom makes great demands upon the technical proficiency of the performer . . .

His versions of the preludes, fugues, toccatas and chaconne, however—which were designed as virtuoso display pieces—are described by Busoni as "arranged . . ." or "freely arranged for concert performance [or "concert use"] on the piano."

Moreover, in time, looking back, Busoni viewed these and other of his Bach and Liszt piano editions, arrangements and transcriptions as part of a self-styled "Advanced School of Piano Playing," a graduated study program that opens with his revised, annotated editions of Bach's *Two-* and *Three-Part Inventions* and *The Well-Tempered Clavier* and concludes with virtuoso transcriptions of Bach's "Chaconne" and Liszt's *Mephisto Waltz:*

> In their entirety [these transcriptions] are similar to an educational building which—preferably with Bach's music as its basis—seems capable of eventually bearing further and younger superstructures, like unto an old, sturdy oak-tree . . . that continues to put forth the greenest and freshest of shoots.

From Busoni's preface to G. Schirmer's edition of the *Toccata and Fugue in D Minor*

Contents

BWV numbers refer to Wolfgang Schmieder's *Bach-Werke-Verzeichnis* [Catalogue of Bach's Works], the standard systematic-thematic reference work for the music of Johann Sebastian Bach. The dates of Bach's original composition and of Busoni's transcription of that work appear below each title.

*In the G. Schirmer edition, Busoni's subtitle for Bach's *Toccata, Adagio and Fugue*. Breitkopf lists the title as *Orgel-Toccata C-dur*.

*authorship considered "doubtful" by *Grove* (1980)

Glossary of German Terms

Many tempo and dynamic markings in these works are given in both German and Italian. Some footnotes supply an English translation as well. Markings in German only are defined below or given their Italian equivalent.

Bässe gehalten u[nd] mit Bedeutung, the bass [line] steady and emphatic
breit, broad

etwas, somewhat, a little

gut gehalten = *ben sostenuto*

mächtig, breit, moderate, broad
mit Bedeutung = *marcato*

nicht eilen, unhurried

sehr breit in Ton und Zeitmass, very broad tone and tempo
sehr getragen = *molto sostenuto*
sehr weich = *molto tranquillo*
schleichend, furtively

Verschieb(un)g = *una corda* ("soft" pedal)

zusammen, together

Toccata and Fugue in D Minor
and the Other Bach Transcriptions

Prelude and Fugue in D Major

(BWV 532)

Original organ work
by J. S. Bach, *ca.* 1708–17

"Arranged for concert performance on
the piano" by Ferruccio Busoni, 1888

Präludium
Moderato

Dedicated to his friend *W. H. Dayas*

Prelude and Fugue in E-flat Major

("St. Anne") (BWV 552)

Original organ work
from *Clavierübung*, Part III, by J. S. Bach, 1739

"Freely arranged for concert use on
the piano" by Ferruccio Busoni, 1890

Preludio.

Moderato maestoso.

+) **NB.** Um die Wirkung des Orgelklanges auf dem Pianoforte annähernd zu erzielen, ist es unerlässlich, dass die Accorde, selbst in weitester Spannung, in allen Tönen zugleich, ohne arpeggieren; angeschlagen werden.

In order to obtain the approximate effect of an organ sound on the piano, it is essential for the chords, no matter how widely spaced, to be played with all notes sounding simultaneously—that is, without arpeggiation.

*) *Sord.* deutet hier und an manchen späteren Stellen die Anwendung des zweiten (Verschiebungs) Pedal an.

Here and in many later passages, *"Sord."* indicates the use of the second *(una corda)* pedal.

Allegro risoluto ed energico.

Toccata in C Major
(Prelude, Intermezzo and Fugue)
(BWV 564)

Organ work by J. S. Bach,
ca. 1708–17, also published as
Toccata, Adagio and Fugue in C Major

"Arranged for concert use on the
piano" by Ferruccio Busoni, 1900

(**1. Preludio,** quasi improvvisando)
Tempo moderato

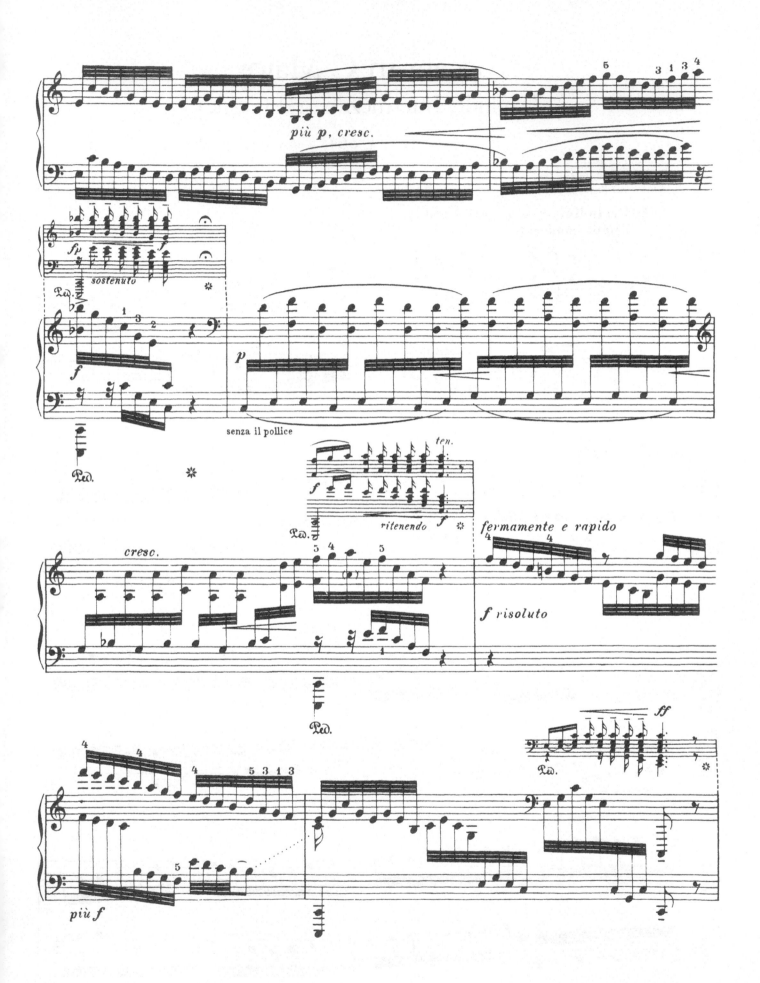

36   *Toccata in C (BWV 564)*

(2. Intermezzo)
Adagio (il Soprano con intimo accento e sempre cantando)

(3. Fuga)

Moderatamente scherzando, un poco umoristico

mf marcato e con precisione, non legato

marc. quasi parodisticamente

Toccata and Fugue in D Minor

(BWV 565)

Original organ work by J. S. Bach, before 1708
published as *Toccata in D Minor*

"Arranged for concert performance on
the piano" by Ferruccio Busoni, 1900

Chaconne in D Minor

From *Partita II in D Minor for Violin*
(BWV 1004) by J. S. Bach, 1720

"Arranged for concert performance on
the piano" by Ferruccio Busoni, 1897?

Andante maestoso, ma non troppo lento
Feierlich gemessen, doch nicht schleppend

72   *Chaconne in D Minor (from BWV 1004)*

82   *Chaconne in D Minor (from BWV 1004)*

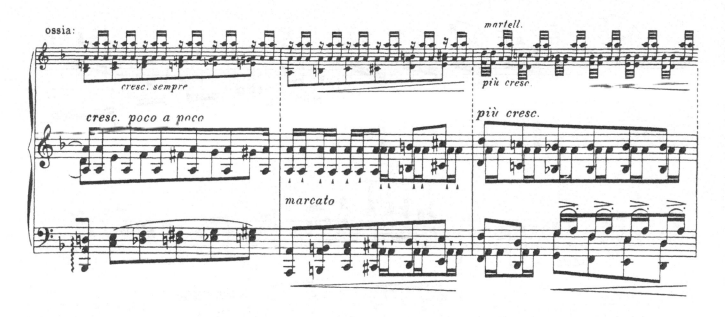

Ten Chorale-Preludes

Original organ works by J. S. Bach "Transcribed for the piano in chamber style"
by Ferruccio Busoni, 1907–09

1. "Komm, Gott Schöpfer, heiliger Geist"
[*Come, God Creator*]
(BWV 667, *ca.* 1708–17)

*) Bei Benutzung der klein gestochenen Noten sind die eingeklammerten auszulassen.
When the smaller-printed notes are used those in brackets are to be omitted.
En cas d'emploi des petites notes, les notes entre parenthèses doivent être omises.

88   *"Komm, Gott Schöpfer, heiliger Geist" (BWV 667)*

2. "Wachet auf, ruft uns die Stimme"
[*Awake, the Voice commands*]

(BWV 645, from the cantata BWV 140, 1731?)

92   *"Wachet auf, ruft uns die Stimme"* (BWV 645)

3. "Nun komm' der Heiden Heiland"
[*Now comes the gentiles' Saviour*]

(BWV 659, *ca.* 1708–17)

*) Das Vorspiel, die Zwischenspiele und die begleitenden Stimmen sollen im Klang gegen den stark zu akzentuierenden Gesang sehr zurücktreten und eine gedämpfte Gleichmäßigkeit bewahren.

The prelude, the interludes and the accompaniment-parts are to be kept well in the background and maintain throughout a quiet, reticent character as a contrast to the melodic part, which must be strongly accented.

Le prélude, les intermèdes et les parties d'accompagnement doivent, au point de vue du son, s'effacer devant le chant très accentué, et conserver une uniformité voilée.

93

'Nun komm' der Heiden Heiland'' (BWV 659)

4. "Nun freut euch, lieben Christen gmein"
[*Rejoice, beloved Christians*]

(BWV 734a, *ca.* 1708–17)

Allegro
Lebhaft und heiter. Die Figuration sehr fließend bei großer Getrenntheit
Molto scorrevole, ma distintamente

"Nun freut euch, lieben Christen gmein" (BWV 734a)

"Nun freut euch, lieben Christen gmein" (BWV 734a)

5. "Ich ruf' zu dir, Herr Jesu Christ"
[*I call on Thee, Lord Jesus Christ*]

(BWV 639, from *Das Orgelbüchlein*, Part III, 1713–17)

6. "Herr Gott, nun schleuß den Himmel auf"
[Lord God, now open heaven's gate]

(BWV 617, from *Das Orgelbüchlein*, Part III, 1713–17)

"Herr Gott, nun schleuß den Himmel auf" (BWV 617)   105

7a. "Durch Adams Fall ist ganz verderbt"
[All is lost through Adam's fall]

(BWV 637, from *Das Orgelbüchlein*, Part III, 1713–17)

Andante mesto
Einförmig klagend

die Figuration sehr gebunden
Legatissime le semicrome

7b. "Durch Adams Fall ist ganz verderbt"*
[All is lost through Adam's fall]
(BWV 705)

Fuga
Molto sostenuto
Langsam

pp (una corda)

Die tiefste Oktave schattenhaft leise
L'ottava profondissima dolce ed oscura

---

*   Dieser Fuge kann das vorhergehende Stück, etwa als Praeludium, unmittelbar vorangesetzt werden.
The preceding piece may serve as immediate prelude to this.

**   Die weiten Griffe dürfen nicht arpeggirt werden.
The wide stretches must not be played arpeggio.

"Durch Adams Fall ist ganz verderbt" (BWV 705)

8. "In dir ist Freude"
[*In You is joy*]

(BWV 615, from *Das Orgelbüchlein*, Part III, 1713–17)

Allegro marcato
Lebhaft, doch gemessen; mit großer Pracht

9. "Jesus Christus, unser Heiland"
[*Jesus Christ, Our Saviour*]

(BWV 665, *ca.* 1708–17)

END OF EDITION